# How To Study In (Almost) Every Situation

*Holly Hassemer*

*Study Smarter Press*

# How To Study In (Almost) Every Situation
*by Holly Hassemer*

Copyright © 2015 Holly Hassemer
Printed by CreateSpace
Published by Study Smarter Press

**Design & Illustration:** Dathan Boardman

ISBN-13: 978-1514278376

ISBN-10: 1514278375

*To Patti, Faith, and Jasmine*
*my Dream Team*

# Contents

When college students are asked how they typically study, the same strategies are mentioned over and over:

- Reviewing notes
- Rereading notes
- Looking over notes

These strategies, while better than nothing, are passive and relatively ineffective. To study more productively and make the best use of your study hours, you have to do something ACTIVE.

To study actively, you should MAKE, CREATE, DO, or SAY something.

This book describes many active strategies for effective studying that can be used and modified to fit nearly any situation. Savvy students will use many strategies in their college careers, varying the ones they use based on each specific discipline, course, and professor. Approach each class and exam independently, identifying which strategies make sense in that situation. There is no one-size-fits-all strategy when it comes to studying—build your study strategy tool box so you are prepared for (almost) every situation.

# Strategies for Almost Any Class

These four strategies can be used in virtually any class to review, process, and retain lecture and text material. They are best used on an ongoing basis. Perhaps you set aside time after each lecture to study with one of these strategies; perhaps you do so once or twice per week. Either way, working with course content on a daily or weekly basis will help you understand and retain information better so you can more efficiently prepare for exams and other assessments.

*Create Study Guides*
*Predict Test Questions*
*Rewrite Your Notes*
*Read Your Notes Aloud*

# Create Study Guides

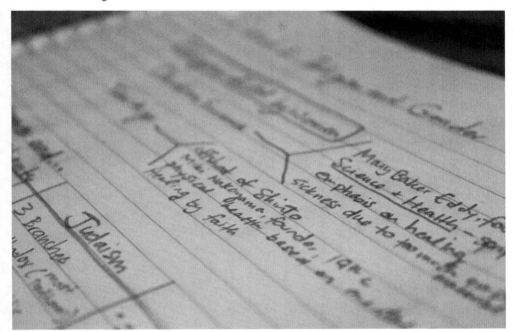

Create a concise (1/2 to 1 page) study guide based on the major ideas from each lecture or reading. Do this by picking out the key concepts, choosing the best examples, and focusing your attention on the most important material covered. Use visual cues like symbols, color, and images to help connect and remember information.

 Create a study guide to review content in a class once per week. If you are uncertain about whether you are picking out the main points or seeing appropriate connections, compare with a classmate or take your study guide to your professor's office hours to get feedback.

Use this strategy to study for any class in which:
- you want to study once per week or more
- there is a lot of content covered and many pages of notes
- there is a comprehensive final exam
- it is challenging to separate the major ideas from the details— better to think about this shortly after class than weeks later when cramming for the exam

# Predict Test Questions

Review lecture notes, readings, or assignments and use them to predict test questions. Think about each major idea, example, concept, or problem and consider how you might be asked about it in the future. Don't be simplistic—your professors will ask complex questions that require deep understanding.

**Even Better** After each class, write down 4-6 possible test questions (with answers) from that day's lecture. Perhaps write multiple questions about the same content to practice thinking about it from different perspectives. Use these sample questions later to study for the exam.

Use this strategy to study for any class in which:
- you want to review after each lecture or reading assignment
- the exams include multiple choice questions—you won't likely predict actual questions, but you will have practice thinking about concepts in complex ways
- the exams include short answer or essay questions

# Rewrite Your Notes

After class (ideally later the same day), rewrite your lecture notes. You can recopy them nearly "as is" or reorganize them in a way that makes more sense to you. Perhaps you take notes by hand in class then type later, or vice versa.

 Add color, symbols, arrows, etc. to enhance the connections between content and create visual cues. Keep two separate notebooks—one for in class and one for your rewritten notes.

Use this strategy to study for any class in which:
- you want to review after each lecture or reading assignment
- the professor jumps around a lot, making your notes messy or disorganized
- the lecture was organized in a way that was confusing to you
- you are provided slides or outlines in advance—you still need to actively process the information even if you have the notes in advance

# Read Your Notes Aloud

Read your lecture or text notes aloud a few hours or days after taking them. As you read, consider the content and note connections you see or areas of confusion. This strategy is markedly better than rereading notes silently—you will be amazed how much better you must understand information to be able to articulate it.

 With a partner or small group, take turns reading the notes aloud. As one person reads, the others add, comment, remind each other, or question the contents of the notes.

Use this strategy to study for any class in which:
- you want to review after each lecture or reading assignment
- the content is challenging and requires some verbal explanations
- the lecture is provided in narrative form
- you have others with whom you want to study

# Reading Strategies

Reading college-level textbooks, journal articles, and other academic sources requires different approaches than other types of reading. Often students just jump to the first page of an assigned reading and begin plowing through the text, working under the erroneous assumption that if their eyes read every word on the page, they should understand the material. This strategy can lead to dozing off, spacing out, and failure to comprehend main points and supporting details. Active reading strategies, on the other hand, keep you engaged and help you process information.

*Underline or Highlight like a Surgeon*
*Take Notes in the Margins*
*Take Separate Notes*

# Underline or Highlight Like a Surgeon

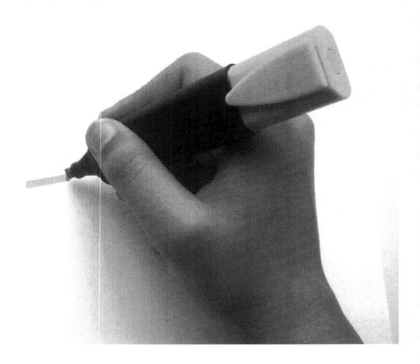

Read with pencil or highlighter in hand (or have the cursor ready). AFTER you read a paragraph, GO BACK and highlight the one or two most important phrases in that paragraph—no more than a few words per paragraph. Just as you don't want a surgeon to cut more than absolutely necessary, you don't want to highlight more than a tiny fraction of the reading material.

 Use this strategy in conjunction with a vocabulary strategy (such as a vocabulary grid) to free yourself from highlighting terms and definitions. Then you can focus on highlighting only main ideas.

Use this strategy for any reading in which:
- you are having trouble focusing or paying attention while reading, but the material generally makes sense to you
- you have the luxury of writing in your book
- you are reading electronic documents, if you can save your highlights

# Take Notes in the Margins

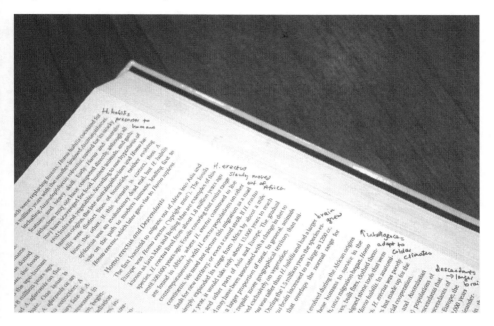

Read with pencil in hand. After you read each paragraph or section, write a few words in the margin to summarize the main point(s) in that paragraph. Then, at the end of each larger section (perhaps a page), write a slightly longer summary of that page's content.

 If reading a textbook that includes paragraph summaries or annotations, take your own notes on each paragraph first and then compare them to the summaries provided in your text book.

Use this strategy for any reading in which:
- the reading is especially dense or challenging, and you need great focus to pull main ideas out of each paragraph or page
- you have the luxury of writing in your book or annotating electronically
- you try highlighting like a surgeon and find yourself still spacing out or getting to the bottom of the page with no idea what you just read

# Take Separate Notes

Read with a pencil and paper or a blank document on your computer at the ready. After you read each paragraph or section, write the main idea(s) into your notes and add any details or examples under these main idea headings. Do this frequently and consistently.

 Enhance your notes by adding color, symbols, drawings, or graphics to allow you to better understand the material. This can be especially helpful if you feel lost in too much text. If your text notes end up being very extensive and lengthy, come back to them later and take notes on your notes.

Use this strategy for any reading in which:
- the organization of the text is confusing to you; organize your notes so you can understand the material
- a deep understanding of the reading is critical for exams or discussions
- you do not have the luxury of writing in your book

# Visual Strategies

Many college courses rely heavily on the spoken work (lecture) and the written word (reading), but many students understand and process visual information more effectively. Don't rely on your professors to provide visuals—create your own! Reorganizing information into a visual format allows you to think actively about information, utilize different parts of your brain, understand and see connections more clearly, and create visual memory cues. Plus, once you create a visual as a way to process information, you can use it again and again for repeated study.

*Create a Chart*
*Create a Concept Map*
*Create a Timeline*

# Create a Chart

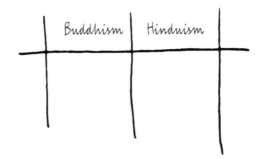

Create a visual that places corresponding elements side by side. If comparing two concepts, this might consist of a two-column chart. If comparing many concepts, the chart will include more rows and columns. Note similarities and differences between concepts on the chart.

 After creating a chart, recite it aloud to memorize it. Then recreate the chart later without notes, relying only on your memory.

Use this strategy to study for any class in which:
- you are comparing two or more concepts, ideologies, people, historical periods, systems, etc.
- you are studying something new and you want to compare it to something you already know in order to understand and remember it better
- it makes sense to systematically compare content presented in lecture and in the text

# Create a Concept Map

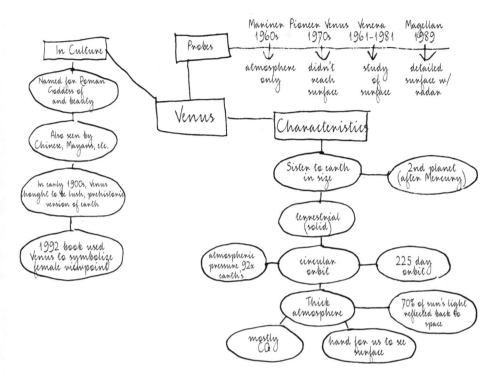

Create a visual that shows the connections between, among, and within concepts using arrows, symbols, and words. Draw out connections that are hierarchical, cause and effect, relational, or otherwise connected. Use words such as "could, avoid, causes, leads to, similar to, sometimes, but, reminds me of, never, etc." to show many types of relationships.

Create your chart by hand or use a software or online program. After creating a concept map, recite it aloud to memorize it. Then recreate it later without your notes, relying only on your memory.

Use this strategy to study for any class in which:
- you want to understand and remember systems and processes
- you want to understand and remember connections between ideas, concepts, facts, dates, people, etc.
- visually processing lecture or reading material is beneficial

# Create a Timeline

| Lecture: Development of Adolescence | | |
|---|---|---|
| Middle Ages 800s-1300s | • Church Discouraged family planning = increased birth rate<br>• Increased mortality (3/5 children died)<br>• little affection toward children - too likely to die<br>• Adulthood started at age 7 or 8 - went to work<br>• married at puberty | Children died or became adults young |
| Renaissance 1300s-1600s | • Rebirth of learning + culture in society<br>• 1693 John Locke → Tabla Rasa (Blank Slate) brains are empty at birth + adults shape them<br>• Theory widely believed | 1st time childhood seen as developmental state |
| Industrial Age 1700s-1800s | • Increase of industrialization + urbanization<br>• children worked in factories<br>• could do work bigger adults couldn't | Children seen as economic assets |
| Modern Age Early 1900s | • Child labor laws enacted<br>• Must be 16 to work in factories<br>• leg compulsory education | 1st time childhood became a legal definition |

Timelines can be excellent visuals—and not just in history classes. Create a timeline to show any information that is chronological or sequential in nature, regardless of whether dates are involved. Even if information is not presented chronologically in class, sometimes rearranging information into a timeline can help you process and understand it better.

 **Even Better** Use graphics and color to enhance your timeline and create memory cues. Create on a computer and copy and paste images off the web.

Use this strategy to study for any class in which:
• content is chronological in nature
• a lecture jumps around  a lot in time and space and it would help you to reorganize the information chronologically
• the sequence of events matters

# Vocabulary Strategies

Understanding and feeling comfortable with new vocabulary can be overwhelming, and it can be easy to spend so much time and effort studying terms that you miss other concepts and connections. Having a set of strategies that allows you to easily handle vocabulary provides you the opportunity to put other effort into understanding key concepts, identifying connections, and analyzing examples. All vocabulary strategies have this feature in common: exposure to the terms over and over and over.

*Create a Vocabulary Grid*
*Talk and Write with Vocabulary*
*Use Flashcards*

# Create a Vocabulary Grid

| Term | Definition (From lecture or text) | In your words | Symbol/graphic |
|---|---|---|---|
|  |  |  |  |
|  |  |  |  |
|  |  |  |  |

Create a grid separate from your regular notes. Make a column for terms and definitions. Add an additional column where you restate the definition in your own words—don't just try to memorize the given definition. Add additional columns if appropriate for the class, such as: examples, pronunciation, or symbol/graphic. As you encounter terms in lecture or text, put the word into your vocabulary grid.

 Fill in your vocabulary grid after each lecture or reading assignment. Then when studying for a quiz or exam, cover parts of the grid and quiz yourself.

Use this strategy to study for any class in which:
- you have a lot of new terms that you need to memorize
- there is a lot of technical or unfamiliar vocabulary that makes it hard to understand concepts in the class
- you are studying a discipline in which you are unfamiliar with the jargon

# *Talk and Write with Vocabulary*

Use new terminology in writing and/or speaking. Do this by engaging in a conversation with a classmate about the topic using the language of the course. Tell your mom or friend all about the content, even if she doesn't care. Talk to yourself on your drive home. Or do the same with writing—write stories, journal entries, or dialogues using the course terminology.

 Talk or write about this course, using the appropriate terminology, over and over. The more you use it, the better you know (and understand) it.

Use this strategy to study for any class in which:
* understanding the ideas and concepts of a course takes more than simple memorization of terms
* there are unfamiliar terms that it is assumed you are comfortable with (make yourself comfortable with them!)
* you enjoy socially studying or using your creative writing skills

# Use Flashcards

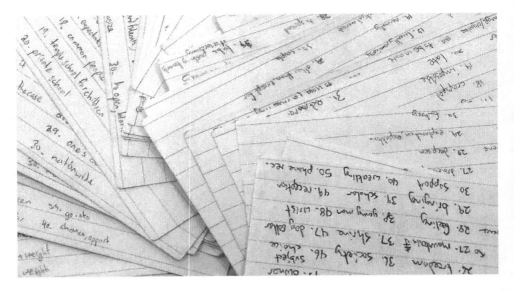

Write a term on one side of a flashcard and the definition or example on the other side. Quiz yourself, ask someone else to quiz you, rearrange the cards, and practice often. Traditional index cards can work, or use a free online flashcard site or app such as www.quizlet.com or www.studyblue.com.

 Keep your notecards simple. If you tend to include too much detail on a card, cut notecards in half to limit what you can write. Color code or use graphics and symbols to categorize similar or related terms.

Use this strategy to study for any class in which:
- you have a lot of terms to memorize
- the terms to memorize are relatively simplistic—complex ideas don't make for good notecard study (use another method!)
- you can carve out short burst of time to quiz yourself with the flashcards—on the bus, waiting for the dentist, on your break at work

# Strategies for Problems and Processes

Many courses, especially in fields such as mathematics and the sciences, require you to solve problems and to memorize and understand processes. Sometimes homework or practice problems are assigned, but frequently just doing problems or looking over processes is not enough. Use active strategies to think about problems and processes in a critical, multi-faceted way instead of simply going through the motions of practice problems. You want to not only be able to do similar problems, you want to understand the concepts behind them.

*Create a Diagram or Flow Chart*
*Create a 3D Model*
*Identify the End Product*
*Recite Steps*
*Annotate Examples in Your Notes*

# Create a Diagram or Flow Chart

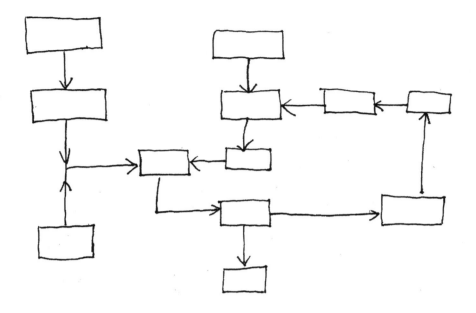

Create or copy a diagram or flow chart that indicates steps in a process or problem. Use arrows or other symbols to indicate progression, alternatives, scenarios, and outcomes.

 After creating or copying a diagram, study it by redrawing it but leaving the information off. Use this skeleton to study by filling in the blanks and quizzing yourself. Then study by starting with a blank page and drawing the diagram itself completely from memory.

Use this strategy to study for any class in which:
- you have to memorize steps in a process
- you have to know the component parts of a process or system in order to analyze, synthesize, or apply them in different situations
- you solve problems in a step by step process, such as Mathematics or Physics

# Create a 3D Model

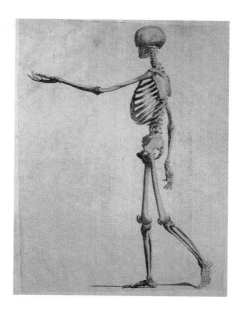

Create 3-dimensional models of concepts, processes, or systems. Use these models by identifying and memorizing the parts, adding or removing parts to walk through a process, or determining what will happen if part of the model changes.

 Purchase a model kit or use any materials you can find: macaroni noodles, colored scraps of paper, Styrofoam balls, paperclips, marshmallows, Halloween skeletons—anything!

Use this strategy to study for any class in which:
- you must understand how something is constructed and/or the working of its constituent parts
- you have to know the component parts in a process or system in order to analyze, synthesize, or apply them in different situations
- the content relates to three-dimensional objects, such as Biology, Anatomy and Physiology, Physics, Chemistry

# Identify the End Product

When determining how to solve a problem, begin by determining what the end product will look like. What units will it be in? What type of information are you looking for? What form will the answer take?

 If the solution to the problem should be x= some number, keep reminding yourself along the way that you are solving for x. Or if this solution should be the number of widgets a company must produce, keep reminding yourself. Doing this can keep you on track and help avoid getting distracted by other numbers or data in the problem.

Use this strategy to study for any class in which:
- you have to solve real world, scenario, or word problems
- you are solving problems that are confusing or require multiple complex steps to solve
- you find yourself getting distracted or off track when working problems

# Recite Steps

When you are learning how to do a certain type of problem or use a formula, recite the steps to solving the problem aloud BE-FORE beginning. By doing this, you focus on the process of solving the problem, not on the specific problem you are working on. Then do each step in turn, saying the step aloud, until you arrive at the end product.

 A simple algebra problem is 3x-9y=12, and you are asked to put it into slope-intercept form. Begin by saying "slope-intercept form is y = something. I solve for y. First I subtract the 3x from both sides. Then I divide both sides by the coefficient in front of the y." Once you have worked through the steps, go ahead and do them.

Use this strategy to study for any class in which:
• you are solving computational problems
• you have to solve real world, scenario, or word problems
• you are solving problems that are confusing or require multiple complex steps to solve

# Annotate Examples in Your Notes

| Lecture Notes | Annotation |
|---|---|
| $4a + 10 = 2a + 26$ <br> $\phantom{4a +10}\; -2a \phantom{=2a+} -2a$ | Move all "a's" to one side by subtracting 2a |
| $2a + 10 = 26$ <br> $\phantom{2a}\; -10 \phantom{=2} -10$ | Move all #'s to other side by subtracting 10 |
| $\dfrac{2a}{2} = \dfrac{16}{2}$ | Divide by # before "a" |
| $a = 8$ | Answer! |

Go back to your lecture notes and look at the example problems presented in class. Using a different color, write the reason for each step next to the example. By doing this you focus not only on specific examples, but on analyzing and understanding the process taken to solve each type of problem.

 Once you have identified common processes to solving problems by annotating examples in your notes, use the flowchart or diagram strategy to draw out the steps to solving each type of problem.

Use this strategy to study for any class in which:
- your lecture notes consist of example after example
- you take notes from your textbook that consist primarily of examples
- computations are a major part of the class, such as Mathematics or Physics

---

*How To Study In (Almost) Every Situation*

# Strategies for Applying Knowledge

While some classes require a lot of memorization, many classes will test you based on your ability to apply and analyze information you have learned. In these cases, simple memorization is not enough. Put your notecards away! You need to study as you will be tested: by using, applying, and working with the information. This may look very different in different fields of study, so listen carefully to your professors and ask questions to help you understand the expectations for applying information in that field.

*Create Scenarios or Case Studies*
*Connect to Prior Knowledge*
*Identify Examples*

# *Create Scenarios or Case Studies*

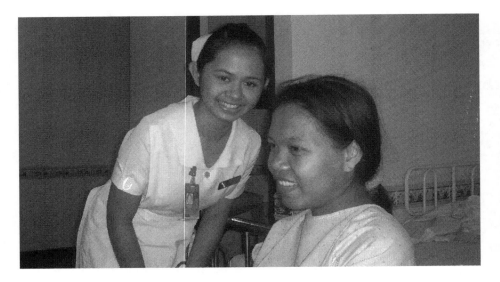

Think of or find scenarios or case studies that illustrate a theory, concept, or idea from class. Consider ways this scenario fits with the theory or things that are inconsistent with it. Start with scenarios presented in lecture or the text, but go beyond those to get additional practice applying theories.

 Compile multiple scenarios and case studies that both fit and don't fit the theory you are studying. Write or explain to a friend, classmate, or tutor why each does or does not fit.

Use this strategy to study for any class in which:
- you have to know a theory and how it applies to real world cases, situations, or patients
- the course content involves complex ideas, concepts, principles, or theories
- you will be tested on the application of the theories or ideas, not just asked to repeat definitions, such as Psychology, Sociology, and Nursing

# Connect to Prior Knowledge

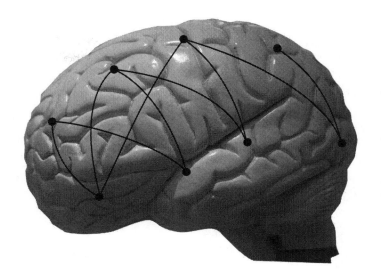

As you hear or read about new information, make deliberate connections between this information and what you already know. How is this new information similar to your prior knowledge? How is it different? How does it expand or build upon something you know? How does this connect to an idea in another class or discipline? The more connections you make, the better you will understand and retain the information because it fits into your existing knowledge base.

Don't just think about connections—get active! Draw them out in a diagram, talk aloud about them, or write them down. This can be a great way to review lecture notes or a text reading.

Use this strategy to study for any class in which:
- the content is new to you—connecting the new content in some way to what you already know will make it more accessible and understandable
- the content is familiar and you already have a strong knowledge base
- the course content involves complex ideas, concepts, principles, or theories, such as Psychology, Sociology, Sciences, Political Science

# Identify Examples

Think of or find examples that illustrate a theory, concept, or idea from class. Or find counterexamples that go against the theory (just don't get them confused with accurate examples!).

 If you are studying different theories of aging, identify people you know or have heard of who fit each theory. Think about your grandparents, celebrities, professors, anyone—as long as you can illustrate (or provide a counterexample to) a theory.

Use this strategy to study for any class in which:
- you have to know a theory and how it applies to real world cases, situations, or patients
- you are working with complex ideas, concepts, principles, or theories
- you will be tested on the application of theories or ideas, not just asked to repeat definitions, such as Psychology, Sociology, Education

25794565R00023

Made in the USA
San Bernardino, CA
11 November 2015